A GIRL HAS NO AGE

D.M. Langdon

D.M. Langdon is also the author of

A Treatise on the Soul (2014),
Universal Wisdom for the Golden Age (2014),
Death Becomes You (2016), and
Dream World (2017).

To order further copies, please visit
www.vividpublishing.com.au/agirlhasnoage

Copyright © 2019 D.M. Langdon
ISBN: 978-1-925846-86-7
Published by Vivid Publishing
P.O. Box 948, Fremantle
Western Australia 6959
www.vividpublishing.com.au

Cataloguing-in-Publication data available from the National Library of Australia

Cover art by Ruby D.L.

Revised second edition. All rights reserved. No part of this publication may be reproduced, stored in a retrieval system or transmitted in any form or by any means, electronic, mechanical, photocopying, recording or otherwise, without the prior written permission of the copyright holder. The information, views, opinions and visuals expressed in this publication are solely those of the author(s) and do not necessarily reflect those of the publisher.

Acknowledgements

I extend my heartfelt thanks to *Reverends Gordon McKenzie and Jennifer Valls* of 'One Light Federation', for whom I have immense gratitude and respect. Thank you both for your incredible depth of Divine wisdom, along with your superb spiritual teaching, inspiration, unwavering support and dynamic spiritual leadership.

* * *

Thank you to *Maggie Bate*, a gifted Medium, Healer and Teacher, for sharing your spiritual wisdom, your loving guidance, your encouragement and your blessings. You really are an amazing teacher and an inspiration to all.

* * *

Thank you to *Nicole McHenry*, a gifted Medium, Healer and Teacher, for your unique teaching and wisdom, your humour, and especially your patience. Your faith in me over the years gives me the confidence to keep persevering.

* * *

Finally, thanks to my family, for whom I am truly blessed, and to my wonderful Spirit team who make all things possible and know me better than I know myself!

Sacred is the truth that calls your name.
Sacred is the new day dawning that seeks
to set love free.
Sacred is the time spent in blissful
surrender to God.
For when the cock crows and the
timing is not right,
this wisdom will lead the way in understanding
the changes that draw near,
the legacy of light, and the future of humankind
in all its glory.

* * *

CONTENTS

Prologue 1

1. Introduction 3
2. A Pathway to be travelled 19
3. A Lesson to be learned 29
4. A Burden to be eased 39
5. A Joy to be found 50
6. A Life to be proud of 61
7. Conclusion 70
8. Personal Message and Prayer 75
   Epilogue 78

Prologue

I was inspired to write this book by Spirit. When I say Spirit, I refer to my wonderful Spirit Guides, the Masters who comprise my Spirit team. They encourage, motivate and heal me. And most of all they love me; pure, unconditional love in all its glory.

I am a Medium and this is the fifth book I've written with the help of Spirit. With my earlier books, I can definitively declare that I was not the author, merely the scribe. The books were comprised of volumes of channelled spiritual wisdom that I received from my Spirit team over several years; wisdom of the highest order as transcribed from Spirit.

A Girl Has No Age is different. Written in my own style, I have sought to combine my own understanding of spirituality using my own expression, merged with the divine wisdom and inspiration provided by Spirit. It is our pure collaboration of the heart and mind. The wisdom provided to me from Spirit has indeed been absorbed by me and has now become part of who I am.

I didn't plan the structure of the book, it just evolved organically as I typed. I had such fun in writing this book. I would type away intensely, get stuck for words, and then Spirit would prompt me. I am not too proud to admit that there were a few occasions when I was prompted with words that were unfamiliar to me, and so I had to consult my thesaurus. Oftentimes, when Spirit provided me with the most striking phrases I needed to pause and absorb the absolute beauty of the words and savour their profound wisdom.

The title is the recommendation of Spirit, and I really do think it is brilliantly suited with its identifiable nod to modern popular culture and its layered meaning. My Spirit Guides really do have a wonderful sense of humour. Initially I was not sure exactly what I should write about, but once the title was provided I knew immediately where to begin – reincarnation and the long, hard journey of our eternal Souls.

I do hope you enjoy this book as much as I do. If you allow this knowledge to seep into your heart and mind and follow the wisdom of Spirit, you really can't go wrong. Herein contains all that you need to know to have a spiritually productive, fruitful and happy existence. And when I meet you on the other side of life, I will be so honoured to know that I made a difference in your life, and I will surely bow to your sweet endeavours of the Soul.

Journey well, and may peace be with you, my friend.

1.
Introduction

I have had many lives. Hundreds.

I say hundreds because to say thousands is mostly unfathomable to me, although I do suspect this number is actually closer to the truth. We are all eternal Souls, after all.

How do I know this?

Well, as a Spiritualist Medium I have had many visions of my past lives; fragments of who I was, what I looked like and, most importantly, my essence of being. These visions were provided to me by Spirit, and they have provided interesting windows into the life of my Soul.

Some visions have also been confirmed by fellow Mediums bringing forth the exact same information at much later dates. In this way, Spirit cleverly ensure we receive confirmation of important information, just in case there is any doubt whatsoever in our minds. This is especially vital if we perhaps suspect that our visions are the result of an active imagination or wishful thinking – indeed, don't we all wish we were Cleopatra?

This information about our past lives, while interesting, is also very instructive. It can give us clues as to what is going on in our present lives and illuminate whatever roadblocks we may be facing. Residue of trauma, pain and non-forgiveness, burdens carried over from one lifetime to the next, and unfinished karma can be ever present in our current life. These energetic burdens can develop into major impediments not just to our happiness, but to our progress on the path to spiritual enlightenment.

Understanding our emotional baggage helps us heal it, rather than burying it, ignoring it, and hoping it will go away. If we deal with it, we can move on with our lives rather than feeling 'stuck' and this brings such relief and a fresh, new outlook on our lives.

Certain talents or preferences may become apparent as a common theme through many lives, as too with aversions. I know writing has been my special interest (talent even, if I may be so bold) carried over quite a few lifetimes. Without a doubt, I am aware there are lifetimes in which I have been killed for my writing, and others where my writing was removed by force and burned.

This lifetime is a new chance for me to get my wisdom to the masses. I understand that if I do complete this task I will find much peace. A feeling of serenity and joy has already started to seep into my very bones as I type these words.

I am also aware, as is the case with many fellow Mediums, that this is not the first life in which I have communicated with the Spirit realms. Thankfully, Mediums living in Western nations are nowadays subjected to generally nothing more serious than ridicule and spite for their gifts, and they no longer face the threat of being burned or drowned for sorcery or witchcraft. This is not the case in other parts of the world, however, where persecution may still occur.

I am aware that not all past life memories are made available to us early on, and sometimes not at all. There are former lives we may never be privy to, especially if they have no real karmic relevance to this one. Also, highly traumatic memories, such as being burned at the stake perhaps, may stop many a fine, young Spiritualist from developing along their path as a Medium. Therefore, attaining this past life knowledge is *all in the timing*.

Divine Timing rules the universe and when the time is right, wisdom is revealed by Spirit for the purpose of the greater good of our Souls. As Mediums, we learn early on to trust that the flow of information provided from Spirit is the right information needed at the right time for the highest good of the person involved, including for ourselves.

Gruesome extinguishing of a physical life can leave negative energetic residue on the Soul, not to mention some interesting birthmarks or medical issues in subsequent lives. These sometimes pop up as gentle and not-so-gentle reminders of horrendous traumas not yet dealt with spiritually. I call them 'energetic imprints'. I suffer an ankle complaint which I understand to be due to an energetic imprint on my auric field caused by a past life trauma. (In the relevant previous life, set in what appeared to be medieval times, I was imprisoned and chained in a dungeon and I had my feet violently hacked off at the ankles.)

When viewed in the context of previous life experiences, issues such as claustrophobia, fear of drowning, a terror of snakes, eating disorders, or various seemingly irrational phobias suddenly become explicable. Some people face what feels like a brick wall, or a breakdown, at a certain age. This too, is no coincidence and the blockage can be indicative of long held baggage from a previous traumatic episode or violent physical passing that has been carried through the Ages unresolved.

Does love at first sight really exist? Well, yes! The instant, deep attraction to another is often a Soul recognition of lives previously shared in love. And what of that person you loathed at first sight, no matter how pleasant? Surprise! They are your old friend and nemesis, a fellow teacher of the Soul, sharing your journey in this lifetime so that you may both have the chance to deal with, and heal, the unfinished business between you. In this way you are intrinsically linked, both parties fulfilling a contract devised in love from the other side. You reincarnate together as part of the master plan to teach each other vital Soul lessons and to help dissolve the karmic burden together.

Now please don't imagine that if you fail a life lesson and have to repeat it you will suffer some sort of 'groundhog day' in the life of your Soul, being shackled and bound to repeat the same painful life scenario over and over. Not so! In subsequent lives, although the Soul group may be the same, the relationships and the scenarios may differ. Your ex-partner in this life may be reborn as your child, your boss, or your mother in the next life you lead (Soul groups reincarnate together over and over), but the vital essence of the lesson and the emotions incurred in resolving the karmic burden between you will be the same.

From my personal experience and understanding based on my insights as a Medium, this unfinished business carried over from a previous life or multiple lives often involves the time-weary life lessons of forgiveness and unconditional love. There are many other lessons of course, and greed is a big one, but in my mind this whole human existence caper called 'life' could simply be renamed as 'The Earth Academy of Forgiveness and Love', because that is why we are here. Simply put, in our short time in this school of life we call Earth we must learn unconditional love to all and forgiveness of those who wrong us. This will ensure we have a joyful, productive life.

What masterclasses are you enrolled in?

Many of us are bound to repeat our lessons on the treadmill of life until we advance to the next stage on our path to enlightenment, inching closer and closer to truly understanding the answer to the age old question – *what is the meaning of life?*

These lessons you are presented with time and again will often involve betrayal, pain or suffering in some form or other. The simple lessons of unconditional love and forgiveness to all will be presented to you over and over in different life scenarios, enabling resolution of any unfinished karma to facilitate progression on the pathway of your Soul. Not forgetting, of course, that you must have unconditional love of yourself. You must forgive yourself for any failures or actions on your part which have caused you pain and regret. It is never too late to change your ways and tomorrow is a new day in the life of your Soul.

Just like any other high-functioning educational institution, we are all provided Tutors while attending the Earth Academy to help keep us on our path of righteousness. And let me make this perfectly clear – it is ALL about *righteousness of being*. To be righteous is to act with integrity always; every thought, word or action carried out with loving grace and compassion to all.

How easy it is to be kind, and yet humankind continues to fail in the simple act of kindness. Not selective kindness to those just like us or those who we can exploit for our own gain, but unconditional kindness to all. Remember, kindness is love in action.

Of course, it is our 'free will' to do whatever we darn well please in life and life is all about *the choices we make*. Take note: that nagging doubt, that intuition, that regret, that inspiration – that is your Spirit Guide, your Master Tutor, one of your own personal team of Spirit Guides and Masters who gently urges you ever forwards on the pathway of your Soul. They are with you always, you are never alone, and they love you unconditionally. Many have been here before, they know the score. They know how difficult physical life on Earth is. They want to ease your burdens and guide you well on your pathway home to God. Welcome them with open arms and open hearts.

* * *

Before you read any further, it is timely for me to note here in the introduction that this book assumes a basic knowledge of spiritual themes which are, by now, fairly well known in popular culture. Nonetheless, I have attempted to clarify a few of the foundational points here which may assist the reader in understanding certain themes or terminology, and ensure there are no misunderstandings.

It is important to remember that each of us has access to spiritual truth, but no-one has the *whole* truth. Even once we pass over to Spirit we do not immediately gain complete understanding of, or unfettered access to, *the full workings of the universe*. Spiritual knowledge has to be earned, on both sides of the veil. Understandably, once we return to the Spirit realms our Earth-blinkers are removed, as it were, and we come to view our life on Earth as if we had been sleepwalking the whole time – blinkered or blind-folded – and not really understanding the point of our existence. On the other side of life we regain access to our previously held wisdom and review and incorporate the latest learnings from our life just led. The *Halls of Learning* are made available to us and we continue to learn and evolve in Spirit.

Sometimes as readers we may come across spiritual concepts that are entirely foreign to us and take us completely out of our comfort zones. It is important therefore to read with your heart and not your head, and really feel what sits well within your heart. It is vital not to dismiss things outright but to ponder quietly, and if you consider that a certain issue is just one step too far for you, then put it gently to one side and consider revisiting it later. Meditate and ask for a sign from Spirit regarding the matter and they will assist you however they can. Do not throw the baby out with the bathwater, so to speak. Do not decide that everything spiritual lacks credibility just because of a few sticking points. I speak from experience here.

The truth of the existence of non-human universal beings is a completely foreign concept to most, surprisingly even to some Mediums. It would seem that talking to one's Grandparents in Spirit is fine, but talking to other beings in the Spirit realms is just a bridge too far for some.

My gaining of spiritual knowledge has been gradual, and I certainly recall that in my early days I considered some issues so fanciful that I failed to entertain them. As an example, I recall that Elemental Spirits (the Spirits closely associated with Mother Nature, such as Fairies, Elves, Pixies and the like) were just never on my spiritual radar. I was therefore sceptical as to their very existence until I saw them for myself. The day a Goblin courteously made himself known to me was a serious wake-up call. My spiritual wisdom has now grown considerably. I understand fully that there are many unfathomable mysteries of the universe and science is always playing catch-up to universal truth. This is the way it has always been, ever was, and likely ever will be.

What is considered dubious to the mainstream now will not be viewed so in the future, and Mediums are certainly doing the groundwork in this regard, in order to raise humankind's consciousness.

It is important to clarify what a Medium does. A Medium is someone who is able to communicate directly with Spirit. This most commonly involves human beings who have died and passed over into the Spirit realms – the astral planes – of which there are many levels. Generally, most Spirit communication occurs in the lower astral planes, with Spirits who have recently passed over, as the energetic vibration is closest to that of the Earth plane.

In this way, Mediums around the world provide a vital service in passing messages from Spirit to those who may be grieving the passing of a loved one. Thus, the mourners are able to understand that life continues after death of the physical body. Life doesn't end; it is simply a change of vibration for the Spirit once the physical vessel is no longer required. This knowledge gives the mourner much comfort.

Mediums also fill many other roles in the service of Spirit, and spiritual healing is a very important one. Some Mediums work in the creative fields of Spirit artwork or channelled spiritual writing. Some Mediums also communicate with Spirit entities who may have never lived a physical life on Earth, such as Angels and non-human universal beings. This is often for the purpose of sharing the profound wisdom of these enlightened beings, including prophecy.

Many universal beings are watching over the Earth with much concern as to humankind's blatant disregard for Mother Nature in all her glory, and our general indifference to the plight of the animal kingdom. Our actions and our apathy are quite perplexing to them. On a whole, I have no doubt that we appear as far less enlightened and evolved than our universal neighbours.

Many Star beings are currently very active in attempting to raise the energetic vibration around planet Earth's atmosphere, as a protective and healing measure. This is because the plight of the Earth is the plight of the universe as a whole. We are all interconnected and if the Earth suffers, the reverberations are felt throughout the universe and have a wide reaching effect.

Not all of our Spirit Guides and Masters may have lived a physical life on the Earth as we know it. Some choose never to be incarnate on Earth, so it is important to remember that we can never make too many assumptions in this regard. The important truth about spiritual wisdom is that we must keep an open mind, always.

Mediums' talents in communicating with Spirit can range from clairvoyance (clear seeing); clairaudience (clear hearing); clairsentience (clear sensing/feeling); and claircognizance (clear knowing). Mediums are often strongest in one of the senses, but are still able to utilise their skills across all. I know some highly gifted Mediums who are accomplished across all these senses and that is a truly remarkable gift. My particular strengths as a Medium are clairaudience and claircognizance.

You may often see the word Psychic used interchangeably with the word Medium, however, they are two different skill sets. A Psychic is someone who is able to read a person's vibrations or auric field and glean much information about them. All Mediums have psychic abilities, but not all Psychics are Mediums. The crucial difference here is the ability to connect with Spirit and obtain information directly from them as the third party, rather than information established intuitively from a person's energetic aura.

When we talk about Spirit we must always

remember that Spirits are energy, pure and simple. They are divine light. And they are genderless. Spirit choose how to present to us in a form we will recognise. This could mean, for example, that they appear to us as their most latest incarnation as someone's Grandmother, even though they do, in truth, have many identities to select from the many lives they have led. Of course, for the sole purpose of passing on a message to a loved one on Earth there is no point presenting to a Medium in a form that no-one still living is able to recognise.

Our Spirit Guides also often present to us in a form we will readily identify with, such as an American Indian, shamanic healer or doctor for healing purposes; or a goddess perhaps, if we are working on balancing our feminine energy. A strong knight or warrior may be necessary to convey strength or protection at a particular time in our lives; or, if we are undertaking important study, a professor might be useful. In this way we are provided whatever quality we may need to tap into at the time, in order to inspire us to pursue and succeed at our life goals, regardless of whether or not our conscious mind realises the presence of our Spirit team.

Many people that believe in reincarnation are of the belief that we are reborn infrequently. From discussions I've had, and from information gleaned from literature and spiritual workshops etcetera, it would seem that the generally accepted period of time between incarnations is around four to five generations, perhaps a minimum of once every eighty to a hundred years or so. Some ancient texts indicate much longer intervals, perhaps every thousand years. These lengthy periods between lives are thought to allow a generous recovery time in Spirit while we learn, plan and prepare for our next incarnation. However, let me assure you without a doubt that this is *not* always the case at all!

Notwithstanding the point that spiritual time is different to Earth time (there is no linear time in Spirit as we know it to be), I am aware of Spirits returning to Earth within the space of between one to five years. In many cases this has occurred within the same family unit, for example, a Grandfather or a Great Grandmother reborn as a Grandchild. Of course it is our free will whether or not to be reborn; a Spirit is never forced to reincarnate. But once in Spirit it appears often to be the case that we are very keen and eager to be reborn on Earth and have the chance once more to accelerate our learning and progress our Soul.

Learning of the Soul can be accelerated when we live a physical life. This is because once we are reborn on Earth our ignorance is at the forefront of our existence. And it is this ignorance of the truth of our eternal Soul and the lack of understanding of the purpose of our life that means our faith is truly able to be tested to the maximum. Making the right choices is harder when materialism and greed lead us down the *corridor of want*. This means our tests in life are much more difficult to understand, and to bear, if we only have our blind faith to lead us to the light. In this way, if God is foremost in our hearts while we go about our life in righteousness, truth, love and peace, then our faith and trust become the accelerants of our Soul's progress.

I believe it is also the case that Souls are reincarnating more frequently because there is much work to be done on Earth at this time. We are soon reaching a crucial tipping point in the history of humankind. The Earth is suffering and the climate is changing. Within less than a century the Earth will be unrecognisable from how it is today. This may explain why many wise, old Souls are currently being reborn (thus clarifying the purpose of the advanced spiritual gifts as seen in the newest arrivals to Earth), and they will no doubt help humankind adjust to a new way of living. In addition, there are many universal beings (both incarnate and disincarnate) here on the doorstep of time, who will assist humankind to navigate and survive the coming changes.

I note from the multitude of spiritual literature available that the terms Spirit and Soul are often interchangeable to the point that many people are confused about the difference. My understanding, based on my channelled wisdom over the years from Spirit, is that our Soul is separate; it is our Spirit which is connected to our physical body. Thus we are an *eternal Spirit living a physical existence on Earth*. This connection of our Spirit to our body occurs any time during gestation and prior to our birth. It is through our Spirit that we gain connection to our Soul, and the exquisite wisdom of our higher self is available for us to access at any time.

Think of the Soul as a repository of all the wisdom and light we accrue over many lifetimes. Equally, the Soul also amasses pain, suffering and sorrow; burdens to be relieved of as we move closer to our enlightenment. Once we reach enlightenment, or arrive at the end of an Age of Humankind (whichever comes first), there will be a unification of Spirit and Soul. Universal salvation and reconciliation; we will be united as one with God and *all that is*.

This separation from our Soul was not always so, but in eons past, we (humankind), bargained with our souls in the Garden of Eden and so here we are, *sans soul* on Earth. Metaphorically speaking, our Soul is now imprisoned, awaiting our redemption. Think of your Soul as the purveyor of wisdom, the source of pride, and a font of harmony and grace, as it patiently awaits the *Coming of the Ages*.

Many often find it is easier to think of the Spirit and Soul as interchangeable terms. In this way, the focus is on the spiritual wisdom provided without the need to get too distracted by discussions around terminology. The main thing is that you believe and trust that you are indeed eternal; that is what is important.

Pedantry regarding spiritual concepts matters not to the progress of your Soul, nor to your successful journey through life. It matters not to the spiritual gains to be made on the pathway of your Soul by living a life of righteousness and grace; and it truly matters not to your ability to live a spiritually successful life of joy, unconditional love and forgiveness to all. You will have mastered life, not theosophical terminology or abstract metaphysical issues. And life is the greatest test of all.

2.
A Pathway to be travelled

We are all of us human (well most of us on Earth, but that's another book), and as humans we are highly emotional beings. The personality, disabilities or circumstances we have chosen for this life when planning our incarnation may be challenging. Overcoming these certain imperfections and learning to love ourselves and find joy in life is all part of the master plan. Nonetheless, do not forget that as children of God we are all perfect in our imperfections – and God has created us thus.

We are all born with a certain degree of mediumistic and psychic abilities as children, but often these abilities gradually retreat as we become accustomed to the norms of the world around us. Children soon learn what is accepted as normal behaviour and what is not, and often their spiritual abilities can become squashed and buried.

For a time, children may live in their own little

world and freely commune with Spirit, usually in the pre-school years (perhaps conversing with Great Grandparents in Spirit or the Elementals in the garden, for example). They quickly learn not to share their experiences with others, even their parents, for fear of the overreaction they generally encounter. Children of non-Western cultures tend to fare better in this regard when it comes to longstanding cultural beliefs in Spirit and the casual acceptance by many of childhood past-life memories.

Once at school, development of the analytical mind and ego usually take precedence and spiritual experiences are often stored away in the recesses of a child's mind until they can barely remember this part of their early life. Development of the ego occurs simultaneously with loss of connection to the universal life force, a separation of self from *all that is*.

When memories do start to resurface they can become like hazy, hard to recall dreams and people often doubt the veracity of their experiences and put it down to an overactive childhood imagination. Even young Mediums who fully acknowledge their childhood experiences with the Spirit realms can find that as they move into adulthood, the harried pace of life or fear of the unknown (or both) often get in the way of their further spiritual development. After all, Earth time is limited and there is much to do!

For most of us (aside from the truly gifted – and believe me I have met these other-worldly Mediums), developing spiritual gifts takes hard work, perseverance, time and dedication. This is difficult to do when stuck on the nine-to-five treadmill juggling whatever drama life throws at you. Beliefs are put on hold until a certain age when time and space allow further exploration of our gifts. It is no wonder that many practising Mediums are well into middle age when they hit their stride. Oftentimes, it is not until any children are grown, work and caring responsibilities are eased, and careers have waned in significance, that spiritualism then finally occupies front and centre position in a person's life.

Not to forget of course that if you are of the quite rational belief that your peculiar talents may earn you the label of someone who is deluded or gullible, then it is, of course, quite natural to both consciously and sub-consciously block communication by Spirit lest you face ridicule and are ostracised by others. A wall is constructed and that wall must then be dismantled.

With maturity comes a certain acceptance and realisation that you are not deluded, only fearful – fearful of the unknown and perhaps fearful of losing your social standing as a rational, sensible adult. Being relegated as weird or deluded is not an easy label to wear.

Regardless, the impetus to be more of your 'authentic self' grows stronger as we age, and the desire to conform at whatever cost is no longer such a driving force in our lives. As we get older it becomes far easier to wear the label of weird or eccentric. With age comes a certain rebelliousness and confidence to finally be who we are meant to be – indeed, who we were born to be. This means no more conforming to society's rules about what is considered to be within the realms of normal.

Women may find their spiritual development pathway easier to navigate than men. This is generally because in our youth and beauty obsessed society that is the Western world, women are often relegated to the ranks of the invisible once they are aged over 50. At this time society often stops policing or, in fact, even noticing the behaviour of older women and this gives them such freedom to finally be their true selves.

From my personal reckoning, men sometimes find it more difficult to gain acceptance of their chosen spiritual pathway from their peers, so all power to them for persevering on their spiritual journey. To develop mediumship skills and connection to Spirit takes courage and fortitude and is no easy feat for anyone. There will be tests and roadblocks for all concerned, doubts and tears, frustration and the utmost joy, but persevere and your life will be blessed beyond imagining. There is no turning back from true surrender to Spirit.

Once you decide to take the first step in your spiritual development journey, your Spirit team will assist in bringing the right teacher or mentor (or even a book) into your life at the right time. You must will this to happen. You must look for the signs (these will be mostly subtle, but sometimes not so subtle) and listen to the guidance of your Spirit team. It is no coincidence that you are reading this book. It was meant to be. I recall being led into a second-hand shop one day on impulse, and my attention was immediately drawn to a spiritual book which I just knew I was meant to buy! So please follow your intuition. Trust that you won't be led astray.

Spiritual signs are everywhere but mostly we don't register. Take note as to what draws your attention – a car sticker, a leaflet, a billboard, a song lyric, a fragment of a dream – there are a myriad of ways for Spirit to get their message across to us in the early days of our development. They want to motivate and inspire us. Your dedication may be tested so it is very important that you don't give up at the first hurdle. Most of all – be patient!

Of course, there is often resistance, but Spirit are not so easily deterred. And if mediumship is part of your master plan of life, you will soon know it. You can only ignore the inevitable for so long.

Oftentimes, Mediums recount having a spiritual 'in your face' moment, and this is orchestrated by Spirit to really get our attention. This is a spiritual wake-up call to finally get us moving along on our chosen pathway, and to follow the master plan we have devised for our life when we planned our incarnation.

Needless to say, mediumship will not be part of everyone's life, although everyone does have some degree of untapped mediumistic ability. Life plans are as many and as varied as there are individuals on Earth. Regardless of our individual life plans, we all have helpers in Spirit and our beloved Spirit team are our cheerleaders of choice. These Masters are with us at all times, guiding, coaching and pulling strings as it were, to ensure we have the best chance to complete our lives with pride, fortitude and blessings from above. If only we will ask them. If only we will let them. Life is all about our intentions and the choices we make.

Free will rules our lives and we have no-one but ourselves to blame if our life is not spiritually fruitful. Our Spirit team loves us regardless. Harness the truth of your intentions and remember that you are eternal Spirit living a physical existence, so act more like your Spirit self – your higher self – and lose the ego which leads you astray. Have goodwill to all others, live in righteousness and truth always, and make choices you are proud of. In this you will be rewarded, with peace and harmony your saving graces.

Younger generations will not face the same hurdles as their older counterparts in developing their connections to Spirit. I truly believe that with each new generation the number of spiritually aware children being born is far greater. In decades to come, it will be perfectly acceptable to the general population to be spiritually gifted. Communing with Spirit will be seen as normal, even ordinary, as more and more children are born with the most incredible spiritual gifts that will be impossible to ignore. They will instead be nurtured and developed and most importantly, they will be celebrated from a young age. This is the future of the human race as I see it.

People will finally have an understanding of Spirit and an acceptance that life continues after the death of the physical body. And by 'people' I mean, in general, people of Western cultures who often lag behind many Eastern cultures in their understanding of Spirit and reincarnation. We are all eternal Spirit. We are all living a physical life on Earth and we are here to learn and to progress our Souls with love. All of us are equal in that regard. We all have burdens to shed, lessons to absorb, and tests to pass on the road to our enlightenment.

Why do we need to progress our Soul and live a life of righteousness? Well, we all have divine light within us, and the purpose of our life – and of living a righteous life – is to embrace and expand our divine light, our connection to God. So be a reflection of your light, as this is the truth of who you really are. This is enlightenment, and the purpose of our enlightenment is to bring us closer to the universal life force; the Divine Creator that is God.

To simplify, there are many levels in the Spirit realms and our growth and learning continues even once we complete this physical life and pass over into Spirit. Nothing is stagnant, all is flux. We need to raise our energetic vibration to the point where we can connect with and progress to the higher, divine light of the Spirit realms. In this way, enlightenment is a continual process, on both the Earth plane and the Spirit planes.

The purification of Spirit and the unification of our Soul; this is the driving force of our Souls, a homecoming to God, our Creator. This anticipated reunion with *the source of all that is* drives us ever forwards, ever upwards on the progress of our Soul.

Every life is progress for your Soul. There are no failures as such, because the Soul grows in wisdom based on the fruitfulness, or otherwise, of your actions, thoughts and words in each life you lead. For every action is a reaction. Energy, once released to the universe via our actions, thoughts and words, cannot be contained. All is recorded in the *Book of Life*.

You create a knowledge bank of wisdom; a reference library for your Soul. The trick is learning to tap into this wealth of wisdom and listen to the higher guidance that is available to each and every one of us via our higher self – our Spirit self. Intention is the key; intention to learn, to grow, to act in *righteousness of being* always and to take the high road in every situation. In all scenarios that you are faced with in your life, the answer is love. It is always love.

Some life lessons are hard to bear, and many kindly and brave Souls volunteer to sacrifice their lives to help us grow. To learn of death and loss, pain and betrayal, joy and suffering, love and forgiveness is all part of the master plan for our Soul's progression to the light.

Every night when we are sleeping our Spirit is safely escorted from our physical body to commune with our Spirit team. Be assured, this occurs even if our sleep is fitful. Spiritual time in the astral planes is different to linear Earth time as we know it, so don't feel you may be missing out if you are an insomniac or restless sleeper. In my experience, to feel your Spirit being escorted from your physical body is not unlike clothing being de-sleeved, inside out, in one long, pulling movement from the body.

When we gather with our Spirit team we conference and we workshop, we review and evaluate, we update plans, renew life contracts and we are nourished with the utmost love and respect that they have for us on our Soul journey. Our Spirit also undertakes special missions of sorts, such as healing tasks, and we are much more active than we will ever realise while our physical body is sleeping. Of course, we are rarely aware of these night time sojourns and our conscious mind is in ignorance of the truth to set us free.

Every Soul journey is sacred and in this way you must never judge another, for you see only the tip of the iceberg in this physical life they lead. You are not privy to their Soul journey thus far; their pain, their suffering, or their sacrifice. So do not judge. God does not judge, our Spirit team do not judge, and in this way we must not judge others but save full judgement for our own selves.

Nothing is random, nothing is chaos. There are no real coincidences in life. All is known to Spirit and your first lesson starts with trusting that this is so. We create the circumstances for the growth of our Soul with our thoughts, words and actions. If you act *in righteousness of being* always, you will be blessed beyond knowing and the hand of God will rest upon your shoulder and lead you to his door. You do not have to be religious or indeed even affiliated with any religion to understand this spiritual truth. The light will lead you home.

3.
A Lesson to be learned

What is your purpose, the main lesson you wish to learn in this life? What lesson plan did you set?

I am very fortunate to understand that a major goal of mine in this life is to spread wisdom about the Soul far and wide, as many are straining for this knowledge. When planning this life, I made a promise to God to pass on spiritual wisdom to as many people as I could reach. In the publication of my books, and the creation of this book in particular, a huge weight has been lifted from my shoulders.

Spiritual wisdom is the antidote to the ills of modern life. Many feel their lives are empty and shallow but cannot put a name on what is lacking, they know only that there is indeed a lack. They notice that no amount of wealth or material goods can fill the hole that niggles and gnaws and grumbles, demanding their attention. No addiction can cure it. No workaholic fervour, excessive partying, or avoidance of solitude can delay the sense that there is something missing, some vital point of their existence. Even fame is only a temporary panacea to the emptiness that erodes. Why are we here? What is the point of our existence?

Writing about the Soul is not my only goal in this life. Like most people, I also have the task of forgiveness of others. I thought I had finished working through my task of forgiveness. When the residual energy of an issue which I believed I'd successfully dealt with resurfaced recently, this took me quite by surprise. I say this to illustrate the point that there is no easy ride for anyone; we all have much work to do. No-one gets a free ride.

In this life I am also focused on healing – healing of others and healing of the Earth – and this is a very satisfying aspect of my life.

I am aware that I have been a male in many of my lifetimes. Another major spiritual goal of mine in this particular lifetime is to bring my masculine and feminine energy into greater balance and harmony, and work more through my heart centre. As Spirit living a physical existence, all human beings contain both energy sources. The feminine energy is healing and nurturing, while the masculine energy is protective and strengthening. Both the feminine and masculine universal energy sources must be in balance for humankind and the Earth to truly prosper.

The Earth at present is struggling and requires much feminine healing light to rebalance itself. Just to be clear, neither energy source is superior to the other but they must be in harmony and at present they are not. The feminine light is diminished and needs to come more to the forefront on planet Earth as she is suffering more than humankind realises.

Sometimes a person's major goal in this life is to learn love – love of oneself. Sounds simple, doesn't it? Who doesn't know how to love oneself, you may ask. Well, please understand that nothing about the human condition is simple. We all have burdens from past lives that we are dragging along in our heart of hearts as a heavy weight. These burdens affect our choices, our patterns of behaviour, our self-worth, our ability to love ourselves and to love one another, and our ability to feel we are deserving of a joyful life. Hearts are heavy, and depression and addictions are on the rise.

Think about how often it is that you hear of celebrities with immense fame and fortune who are so unhappy they feel they cannot continue living. They take drugs to excess to ease their spiritual emptiness or may even suicide to escape from the pain of their lives. Many observers simply cannot understand why these people could possibly be unhappy as they seem to have it all in our materialistic, celebrity-obsessed culture.

To believe that fame and fortune will provide happiness is deluded, and yet we continue to see hordes of fame-obsessed people courting celebrity via social media or reality TV stardom. Some are so desperate for stardom as an acknowledgement and validation (or even distraction) of self that they resort to seeking recognition by becoming the latest purveyor of outrageous social commentary on various platforms. Notoriety is increasingly gained through shock tactics. They spurt off deliberately perverse, hateful and controversial views, anticipating a media stir which may lead to world-wide fame. It is not freedom of speech they seek, but admiration from others, validation of self and the courting of unconditional love from the public for a self so damaged they see no other option but to test the world thus.

Unfortunately the dangerous end point to all this attention seeking is when outrageous words become outrageous actions. And innocent people are killed.

On the subject of fame and wealth let me make this perfectly clear – fame and wealth are never the problem. It is greed, pure and simple, that will erode the Soul of happiness and growth. There are many wealthy people and this is but one test of life – how to be happy and live in *righteousness of being* with the burden of wealth. And yes, it is a burden for it brings with it many responsibilities. My Spirit Guide described it powerfully when he said: 'In ignorant bliss of the days that are numbered we go forth dragging the entrails of our materialistic life behind us.'

Those who harbour greed face a major obstacle in the growth of their Soul. Understanding that material wealth is worthless in the land of your Soul is a key accomplishment in a materialistic world. Of course, it is essential to be generous with money and material goods to those less fortunate if and when we can, but it is also generosity of time, unconditional love and understanding that is required. To give of our time to the lonely and bereft is indeed a precious gift that can be bestowed by the wealthy and the poor alike.

There are multitudes of wealthy people who are kind and generous, and greed plays no part in their life. Such advanced Souls understand that life has its ups and downs and they have undeniably been fortunate to be able to live a life of relative comfort. They are grateful for the circumstances of their life. They do not blame others less privileged for their misfortunes, understanding that the wheel of life turns and you cannot always be guaranteed a seat at the top of the wheel.

Some lives are jam-packed with spiritual lessons and tasks and much wisdom is to be learned. Many lives may involve horrendous suffering and sorrow where the learning is accelerated. Other life plans may be more subdued. Perhaps a sacrificial support role to another's spiritual growth is your role of choice? Perhaps only minor lessons are required in this life so as to prepare for the next life in which a major milestone is on the agenda for your Soul's growth. This means enormous progress for your Soul is in the offing. Please remember that no matter how short your life is, growth is always assured.

There is no stock standard contract in life; all life plans are tailor-made for the best outcomes possible. What you do with these opportunities for growth is, of course, entirely up to you. We all have free will which can be both a blessing and a curse, as many are easily led astray by their ego.

Do not make the mistake in thinking that some lives are more worthwhile than others. This is a judgement made through a non-spiritual lens and usually based on humankind's values of wealth, power, beauty and success. To live a life of joy, unconditional love to all and forgiveness of all those who wrong you – unassuming as your life may be – is the sign of a life well lived and a Soul well served; a very successful life, indeed.

So what is your major lesson in life? What theme keeps presenting on your pathway? Who or what is it in your life that currently causes you grief? Current or residual pain should give you a clue.

The lesson you face with your antagonist/s (or even yourself) may perhaps involve betrayal, pain or non-forgiveness in some form or other. Some circumstances may be minor. Others may be major transgressions – hardships for the Soul of the highest order. The lesson of providing unconditional love and forgiveness to those who wrong you will recur over and over in each life you lead, until you make the grade. Acceptance of this truth will see you proud.

Revenge and hate are a heavy burden for our Souls to bear. There is an old proverb attributed to Confucius which states, 'before you embark on a journey of revenge, dig two graves'. This is because hate is poison to our Souls and if we harbour animosity and thoughts of revenge we can end up destroying our own lives in the process. We need to release the hate, forgive and move on. Hate is anathema to the Soul. It lowers your vibration and the negativity surrounds you like a fog. Your heart becomes heavy and the pain is magnified.

True forgiveness from the heart is required, not pithy words of insincerity uttered simply to gain the higher moral ground. It must be sincere and heartfelt. Forgiveness does not mean you are diminished or a doormat. Forgiveness is not a sign of weakness. It does not mean you condone their actions or allow toxic people who have wronged you to remain in your life. Nor does it mean that you fail to report a crime or make excuses for unethical behaviour. It simply means forgiving their actions and moving on. Release the energy to the universe via your intentions and your prayers, transmuting it to love and light in wisdom and in grace. This will resolve any unfinished karma between you and enable progression on the pathway of your Soul.

Forgiveness does not simply mean 'forgive and forget', as the saying goes. Forgiveness requires emotional action, not passivity or inaction. Forgiveness is unconditional love, not numbness or neutrality of emotion. You will know you have succeeded in your quest to forgive when you can think of the situation and remember it without prevailing bitterness.

And what to do if your pain is caused by a failure

to gain forgiveness from someone you yourself have wronged? Forgive them for being unable to forgive, and move on. Forgive yourself for your misdeeds – your actions, thoughts or words. It is never too late to redeem yourself. All is not lost, so never believe you are a lost cause. There are no lost causes in the journey of our Souls. Pray for forgiveness and vow to live in love and harmony from this point forward. Never look back, do not dwell in the pain of the past. If you learn from the errors of your ways then your life has truly been fruitful. Move forward, ever upwards and onwards to the light of your redemption.

Think of the many great Master Souls who have graced the Earth and set the finest example of love and forgiveness. Jesus came to Earth to show us how to live so that our Souls would prosper. His life is a prime example of forgiveness in action. Jesus forgave the great injustices inflicted upon him and loved everyone unconditionally. His life continues to influence millions to this day and he is a beacon of hope to all who follow in his stead.

Jesus loves us all unconditionally, even when we forget to love ourselves. The divine Christ Light that Jesus brought to the world nourished and soothed. Once again, Jesus and the Christ Light will be viewed across the Earth; this knowing a blessing for all who understand *the time is nearer to our Souls*. We await the day of true harmony and peace.

Many fine Souls have followed the example of Jesus, our Master teacher, and sought to live a life of love and forgiveness. There are many in recent recorded history and Nelson Mandela immediately comes to my mind as a very wise, old Soul. He showed us how to forgive and live in unconditional love of others. His life path was very rocky indeed but he surely graduated with the highest honours from the Earth Academy of Forgiveness and Love. Such an esteemed alumnus!

Remarkably to most people, there are survivors of atrocities such as the Holocaust and other genocides and tragedies who have been able to forgive their tormentors – the slaughterers of their people, their brethren and their families. This is not an easy path to take but after much heartache and soul-searching these incredible individuals come to the understanding that the hate and the pain they carry is eating them alive. They know the best way to move on and to have peace in their life is to forgive their enemies, despite the horrors they endured. These wise Souls are truly advanced on their pathway to enlightenment.

You may think that your suffering doesn't count. You may feel that it is petty and self-absorbed to feel hurt and suffering over some workplace betrayal, family division or broken heart, compared to what other poor Souls may have endured in their lives. Surely, in comparison, a seemingly minor betrayal of the heart couldn't count as such a test, could it? Well, yes. Please be assured that *all* suffering is a lesson for the Soul and people are tested in many, many ways. It's just that some fine Souls have elected to take masterclasses, an acceleration of sorts. This may not just be for their own growth, but also for the purpose of consciousness raising for humankind as a whole. Such generosity of Spirit!

Your pain and suffering is a chance to pass a test of forgiveness and unconditional love, so do your homework, make the grade, and you will be rewarded. When you eventually pass over to Spirit you will look back on your life with such pride and joy, having advanced your Soul with wisdom and grace. What joy! What an honour! Your Spirit team will be ecstatic, the Angels will sing and you will understand the purpose of your life just completed, the knowledge gained, and the strides made in the progression of your Soul.

Your life wasn't fruitless. It was productive and rewarding and you will be so excited to return to Earth to do it all again and progress to your next class in the Earth Academy of higher learning for the Soul.

So never fear the death of the physical body. When the time comes you will be happy to shed your body – your garment of choice – like an old, heavy overcoat that has served you well. You will not look back. Our real home is in Spirit and you will feel such a sense of home-coming when you do arrive. Think of life on Earth as being at a boarding-school. Between school terms – between each separate life you live – you get to go home to the Spirit realms for the holidays to refresh and renew, see old friends and loved ones, and eagerly await the start of the new school term on Earth in the new school 'uniform' of choice.

4.
A Burden to be eased

I have mentioned already that key learnings for the Soul often involve love and forgiveness. To act in unconditional love and forgiveness to all who wrong you is the pinnacle of human achievement. To live in *righteousness of being* provides true harmony between body, Spirit and Soul. And we must remember always that life is a privilege and we should not squander it.

Many times people may say 'I didn't ask to be born'. But indeed you did, and the key circumstances of your life on Earth were orchestrated by you before you were reborn. Do not shift responsibility for any misfortunes you may face onto someone else, or even onto God. Instead, reflect within your heart in quiet contemplation and count your blessings daily. Vow to live the best life you possibly can, despite whatever circumstances bring you pain. You reap what you sow. If you live in harmony and grace, with love for all *despite* your harsh, difficult life, you will be blessed beyond knowing. If you choose hate, spite, fear and sorrow as your daily garments of choice then you will simply attract more of the same into your life.

Tomorrow is another day in the journey of your Soul. Make every day of your life count. The day will come when you realise that the summer of your life has waned, and the winter of your life brings the quiet realisation that time on Earth is precious and not a day should be wasted in negativity, self-pity and hate.

Seek to improve whatever circumstances are bringing you pain, and above all pray to God and ask your Spirit Guides to help ease the burdens that weigh you down. Think of prayer as a personal conversation between you and God, the Master Creator. You do not need an intermediary, a church, or any other place of worship to be close to God. You will find him in your heart, always. All prayers are heard. If you do not receive answers to your prayers it is because whatever you have asked for may not be in the best interests of the higher purpose of your Soul's journey. As you will not be aware of the bigger picture or plan, you must always trust that this is so and believe that you are in wise hands.

This is not to say that there will be no result at all from prayer. All prayer, if sincere and heartfelt, brings a healing response but you will rarely be privy to how this plays out on an energetic level. If you pray for someone who is gravely ill but who passes over to Spirit despite your supplications, be assured that your prayers will have made their passing so much easier.

Pray for yourself and others and especially pray for Mother Earth. Thoughts and words have form and energy in Spirit, although this is a concept we humans oftentimes find hard to imagine. Once you return to Spirit you will be able to see the energetic vibration of your prayers with your spiritual eyes, in a manner of speaking, and you will be astounded that this energy from your mere thoughts took such a healing form of light and love, visible to the universe. You will, without a doubt, wish that you had prayed more often when you see the results of your ministrations.

Bring positive energy and good intentions into your life and remember 'like attracts like'. If you act against your conscience and wallow in self-pity, ill-will and hatred of others you will drown and choke in the dark mire of your bitter existence. You create the circumstances of your life by your thoughts, words and actions, so make sure they are of the highest energetic vibration of love – love of self, love of others, love of God, love of Mother Earth and of all God's creatures on it.

You cannot love God if you do not love yourself, as God is within us all. We have each a spark of God's divine light. We are all of one light; we are one universal light. The many divisions we create between ourselves as human beings are false edifices that do not exist in Spirit.

Life is an adventure. A key lesson of life is that we must also find joy in all that we do and in the way we live our lives. Joy of living is the greatest expression of gratitude to God. Life is not meant to be austere and joyless. Life is a blessing, a joyous ride. It is to be savoured. It is all about appreciating the simple things in life. Simplicity is the key. We all complicate our lives unnecessarily. Many of us fill it with mountains of material goods that we will never need and money that we will never spend. We try vainly to make our life seem worthwhile, one futile acquisition after another. But the more we accumulate, the emptier we feel, and the less satisfied we become.

Some may decide by their own hand to check out of the Earth Academy early, in many cases derailing their life plans. Be mindful of course that suicide may be part of their master plan to teach others of the pain and heartache of premature loss (but of these sacrificial Soul teachers we can never really be sure).

There are many different ways we all manage to sabotage or derail our life plans, in small ways and large. People are very creative when it comes to devising their own self-destruction in a world of pain they cannot deal with, be it a quick death or a lingering, downhill slide to their oblivion via the addiction or heartbreak of their choice.

Suicide is a free will choice, often acted on when the pain of life becomes too overwhelming and the burdens too heavy, and this is truly saddening. Life is all about the free will choices we make, and God has given us this autonomy so we can truly learn and grow in wisdom and be proud of our choices in life. However, we must not judge another's choices as Spirit do not judge. Much spiritual healing is provided to the dearly departed in the Spirit realms and Spirit work diligently to ease the pain and provide understanding, wisdom and loving guidance.

Many a Soul prematurely departed is back on the rollercoaster of life in the heartbeat of time, ready for another shot at life in a body of their choice. Born to parents of their choice in the life of their choosing, they are all set to complete their Soul lessons once again. The cycle of life goes on.

A common refrain to the injustices of life is 'Why would a loving and just God allow this?' It is tempting for people to disregard God as a fallacy of simple minds when there is so much hardship and suffering, people are starving, and children live in poverty or war. The simple answer is that God allows this because he gave us free will. We bargained with our Souls many, many eons ago and this is the inheritance of humankind.

Life only seems unjust if viewed from the standpoint of a *singular life* and the stark, cruel inequality of the world, especially for those born in circumstances deemed less fortunate than our own. Of course, now you know that this is not the case at all. The cycle of life is indeed just, no matter if born a pauper or a princess. We all have many, many lives. We are born into different races, creeds and genders, with differing conditions to learn under.

Our life continues after death and we all take our turn aboard the *Wheel of Life* to suffer and to grow in wisdom of the Soul.

Free will rules our lives in both this world and the next, and enables us to make choices we are proud of. Every situation on planet Earth is of humankind's own making; the future brings what individual and collective decisions have sown. God can intervene and has intervened, and he will no doubt continue to intervene in small ways and large but mostly we will be unaware (unless by way of verified miracles). However, the rest is up to us. This is another test of life – *individual responsibility* for our own actions, thoughts and words.

When people come into your life and cause you anger, pain, discomfort or sorrow, please know that they are your teacher and have a valuable Soul lesson to impart. Is it patience? Is it acceptance? Is it forgiveness? Is it individual strength? Perhaps the lesson of the day is simply to learn to rise above pettiness and spite. It may be to humbly walk in someone else's shoes for a day, a week or a month to understand more fully that no-one's life is ever easy. This may be your chance to let go of any bigotry and narrow-mindedness.

Everyone has wisdom to share of some worth, no matter how uneducated. There is the education that is received in school, and then there is the education received in the school of life – these are two completely different curricula!

Every obstacle or road block that presents on

your life path in the school of life on Earth is a chance to grasp an opportunity to grow in wisdom of the Soul. Relish the chance to progress upon your Soul path, with love and kindness at the forefront of your daily existence.

Hatred of the 'other' is a sorry state of humankind. When people deliberately kill or harm another, there grows a cloak of sadness they wear like a shroud. Their arrogance their armour, they deny their troubled heart till it is near to bursting, their pain refashioned into a badge of honour. The pain of regret buried deep in their heart is second only to the anticipated pain of their deliverance. Hatred of the 'other' is a lonely song to sing, the epitome of ignorance and fear.

Once in Spirit, these pitiful Souls are set to learn of wisdom, pure and true. With mercy and tender loving care they are shown the harsh reality of their lives. (Think here of suicide bombers, mass murderers, tyrannical despots, and the like.) They view their actions mired in hate; the pain and suffering they caused reverberating through the universe. They realise the heavy burden on their Soul. If they accept the truth of their being and repent the stench of their life's foul choices they are of course redeemed, and they work to gain suffrage for their Soul. All is forgiven. We are always loved and we are always forgiven; do not ever doubt this truth.

Acceptance of the truth of their existence is not an easy path. Much healing is provided in Spirit to those who have committed such evil acts, and this helps them to acknowledge their ignominy as a child of God. Any resistance to this truth is but a transitory limbo of their own making, with their Soul temporarily trapped in stasis. But all is not lost. When the time is right and their Spirit is ready, they will see the light and surrender to the joy of their redemption. They understand the truth to set them free. Such joy to behold! They may then elect to return to the Earth Academy of Forgiveness and Love, in the *remedial class* of their choice.

Thus life is a veritable game of Snakes and Ladders. We climb and we fall and it is our free will choice to pick ourselves up, forgive our sins, and continue along the long, hard journey of our life, complete with the frequent flyer points of the Soul and the excess baggage of the Ages.

As a Medium, many of the messages I provide to people from their loved ones in Spirit relate to regrets – the regret of things done or not done and the regret of things said or not said. Regrets generally encompass common themes, such as not telling their loved ones how much they loved them, or how proud they were of them. Often they wished they had given them more of their time, money, understanding, respect or compassion. Disappointment in the failure to reconcile with loved ones, friends or business partners before their time on Earth was up sits heavy on many a Soul.

Many loved ones in Spirit indicate they are truly sorry for whatever incident or issue may have remained unresolved at the time of their passing. It is such a waste to be disenfranchised from loved ones over Earthly issues involving things like money or egotistical pride. Once in Spirit they realise how insignificant their trivial squabbles on Earth are in the greater scheme of things. They also realise how much pain they may have caused others when they view the full, unedited production of their life.

Understandably, there is such emotion and spiritual healing when these messages are conveyed from the Spirit realms, but wouldn't it be much better to pass over with a clean slate, so to speak? After all, there are very limited opportunities for Spirit to get through directly if their loved ones are not attuned to the energetic vibration of the Spirit world.

Thankfully, most Spiritual Churches conduct 'evidence of survival' or the similarly named 'proof of life' mediumship demonstrations as part of their regular services, whereby Mediums relay messages to audience members from their loved ones in Spirit. There are many in the Spirit realms who clamour to get a message through to their loved ones still living, but unfortunately not everyone can receive a message as Earth time is limited and the Medium only has a short window of opportunity to work with. So while many in the audience may be disappointed to miss out, there are just as many, if not more, in the Spirit world who have queued – for want of a better word – unsuccessfully to get through to the Medium with a message to pass on. Disappointment all round may be palpable. It stands to reason then that it would be much easier for all concerned if important sentiments, such as remorse, were expressed while still on the Earth plane. Hindsight is a wonderful thing of course, and it is better late than never.

Words of apology and contrition, once expressed, have a healing quality if given always with the best intentions of love and understanding. The Spirit teams act as gatekeepers to this process. Of course some messages may not be accepted by the intended recipient at the time. They may be dismissed or disagreed with. They may be rejected and thrown back in vitriol, but nonetheless, they will start an energetic chain reaction that will provide much healing. After all, it is far better to nurse and nurture these words than to speak harshly of their absence. And in this way a precious gift is provided – a gift which engenders forgiveness and understanding whilst still in the physical. This is a tremendous gift from Spirit. It is an opportunity for the recipient to release a karmic burden, but only if the words are taken into the heart with true acceptance, unconditional love and forgiveness.

Individually and collectively we all have karma which impacts how we live our lives. Nations have collective karma and planet Earth too has karma. Planet Earth has its own Soul journey to make and is suffering greatly under humankind's stewardship, but this too will continue to play out as we are currently witnessing. Natural disasters will increase in frequency as the Earth seeks to rid itself of toxic burdens and cleanse itself of humankind's legacy. The dire global environmental consequences caused by the impacts of the selfish greed of humankind will be a hard lesson to learn. The animal kingdom is aware of this impending doom and likewise many a fine Soul can already see the writing on the wall.

5.
A Joy to be found

There are many mysteries of the universe, many more than our Earthly minds can even begin to fathom. Scientific knowledge grows in leaps and bounds and when the time is right, the relevant knowledge is communicated by Spirit to the elected person, at the elected time, as part of the master plan. This communication can occur in many forms, but generally a dream or a thought pattern is imparted on the conscious or subconscious mind and thereby the wheels are set in motion. Many great scientific minds choose to be the carrier of the wisdom of the day, as science plays catch-up to spiritual truth.

Humankind is not yet ready to learn of universal beings from other star systems or the vagaries of spiritual time, space and energy, and other universal wonders. These unfathomable mysteries keep the Spirit realms (often times referred to simply as heaven) safely out of mind and out of touch to most human beings, even to the most dedicated of quantum physicists. And when I say 'out of touch', this is not because heaven is in the sky, so to speak. Heaven is actually among us, around us and within us. It is all about compatible energy vibrations. If only we could all open our hearts and feel this heavenly vibration. We need to go within to find God and connect with the Spirit realms. Most people mistakenly think they need to search externally for answers.

When we talk of Spiritual time it is important that you are aware that spiritual time is not linear like Earth time, otherwise nothing about the Spirit realms will likely make sense to you. In Spirit, all our many lives are being lived simultaneously; *there is no 'then and now', only 'is and ever was'*. This is a very hard concept to fathom, but just trust that this is so. This is why some advanced Mediums can tap into a person's future lives as well as their past lives ('future' and 'past' only in the sense of our linear Earth time), as all our lives are occurring concurrently on different planes of existence. We can tap into these lives if our energetic vibrations are compatible, but only if there is a greater purpose to be served by this knowing.

Throughout the centuries of the recorded history of humankind, many different cultures and religions have historical written or oral records which indicate a belief in Spirit. History is full of doctrines and texts indicating the belief in the afterlife and the ability to communicate with the divine Spirit realms, as well as an acceptance of reincarnation. Some records advocate the ability of a person's Spirit to leave their physical body temporarily (astral travel) to bask in the higher light of the divine, returning with much wisdom for their people. Shamans, Siddhas, Buddhist Monks, Jewish Mystics, and Prophets of all creeds in abundance – this belief in Spirit is certainly not merely a recent New Age phenomenon as often portrayed.

In more recent times, we are hearing more and more about near-death experiences. This may be due to advances in modern medicine which have enabled more people to be brought back from the brink of death. There are many near-death survival stories where survivors of all backgrounds and ages have recounted the sensation of their Spirit leaving their physical bodies, often while medical staff are working to resuscitate them. Many describe similar occurrences, such as being drawn to a tunnel or a bright light, experiencing astral travelling, or communicating with loved ones or other beings in Spirit. People are now curious. Many are becoming more and more open to the possibility that there is much more to life and death than we could possibly know.

There is also an increasing popularity in seeking out past-life regression treatments where people undergo clinical hypnosis to try to understand and deal with their various current life issues, including unexplained phobias and health issues. This is usually after common medical and therapeutic methods have failed to make progress. There is a growing body of published works which include detailed case studies of near-death experiences and past-life regressions, and these go some way in quenching people's thirst for spiritual truth and understanding.

Thankfully, as the energies around the Earth continue to shift causing a change in vibration, many more people are spontaneously awakening to Spirit and becoming open to this higher energetic frequency. Many sensitive people, especially the young, are intuitively connecting to this higher energy field and receiving a 'spiritual download'. In this way, there is a gradual raising of humankind's collective consciousness.

Many religious institutions are mired in dogma – manufactured, man-made precepts based on historical scriptures warped and corrupted over time due to errors in translations, fanciful editing and deliberate omissions by the powers of the time. (How do I presume to know this? The clue to this is as was stated in my Introduction – I have indeed been a writer in many lives and across many faiths.)

There is many a truth between the biblical lines of old, but please be aware that it is certainly not *the whole truth and nothing but the truth*. That said, the most fundamental and important messages of religious scriptures and ethical texts are all very similar. Tenets such as: love thy neighbour as thyself; do no harm; and do unto others as you would have them do unto you; and so on and so forth, represent solid, indisputable wisdom of the Ages which no-one can deny.

There are countless fine people of various belief systems and religious congregations who are sincere in their compassion and love of others. Leaders and followers alike, they spend their days helping the less fortunate in many practical ways, their kind hearts worn on their sleeves. These people are to be applauded and their selfless acts are truly remarkable. They are noble Souls who have based the principles of their life on the example set by the great Masters.

However, when religious dogma is used to justify inequality; when power, status and control become the driving forces; when abuse is rife and compassion is lacking then, sadly, hypocrisy abounds. When wealth is squirrelled away by the upper echelons of institutional power who put more creative thought into how *not* to spend their billions than to help the needy of the world, then religion has clearly lost its way as the moral compass of our time.

Many non-religious unbelievers live their lives in utmost moral rectitude and this is to be celebrated. These quiet achievers of the Soul go about their lives with no need for grandstanding or fanfare. Their Spirit Guides continue to rally, prompting them when they can. These doubters are secure in the comfort of their higher selves who lead where they would follow. Imagine the joy they would feel if they knew of the unbounded pride of their Spirit team basking in the triumph of their righteous existence. Many make the journey and this is a difficult test of life. To act morally and in *righteousness of being* with no guiding star to light the way – to recognise that you were your own leading light all along – is exquisite learning for the Soul.

We are all born wanting to live a good life but often we find we end up derailed, the circumstances of our early life setting us off on many a detour from our desired pathway. To rise in triumphant glory from a childhood of hardship and cruelty; to rise above hatred and neglect, pain and abuse to treat all others with the care and dignity that we so often lacked is true splendour of the Soul, a doctorate in the lesson of love. This is a truly remarkable achievement.

To drown in the harsh reality of a life spent in pain and suffering and to lash out at others to ensure their very same fate, is a particular horror borne of humankind. Regrets are many and the pain is ongoing; there is no respite from the fear and horror of a life forfeited to hate, anger and sorrow. The wounds are deep, the echoes of the Soul reverberating beyond the chamber of our feeble existence. These Souls are lost, but still redeemable. There is much work to be done. And still the Soul learns, in this life and the next. Our free will carries through, and first and foremost when we pass over and return to Spirit we must accept the truth of our existence. No denials, no blame on others, just an understanding of the truth to set us free – it was *our* journey, *our* ticket to ride, *our* free will choices.

My Grandfather was a wonderful man. He was brought up a very strict Catholic and was bombarded with the social and religious doctrines of his generation which he rejected as a young man when he chose to marry for love. Over time he developed his own personal relationship with God and he was comfortable with the innate knowledge that God loved him unconditionally. He understood that he needed no formal institution to maintain his relationship with God. No power broker of the heart, no intermediary or bursar of the Soul was required, just a personal connection to God within his heart and his own lived example of a compassionate and spiritually fruitful life. He was a kind and loving man who endured constant physical pain due to a serious bone injury in his leg from a horse riding accident when he was a young adult. In his later years he did have some relief when his damaged leg was finally amputated.

I am aware through communication with my Grandfather in Spirit that aside from the usual issues of forgiveness which most of us are faced with at some time in our lives, a major lesson of his life for the growth of his Soul was to learn of pain – physical pain of the highest order. The constant pain of his damaged leg bone throughout his adult life was an entrée to the pain of his death.

When my Grandfather passed over, aged ninety, from a major stroke some decades back, his suffering was immense. He was in a coma for a week as his organs gradually failed. In more recent years he has allowed me the great privilege of seeing (clairvoyantly) that when his pain was too much for him to bear, the Angels of Mercy periodically lifted his Spirit out of his body so he could gain respite from the worst of his suffering. At the time, we were completely unaware of this pain, as was his wish. Due to the intervention of the Angels of Mercy, not only did he gain respite from the pain, but he also felt the ecstasy of the proximity of God.

It would be easy for me to wallow in the grief that the knowledge of his temporary suffering brings to me. However, I understand that this was a Soul lesson he chose to complete in the lesson book of his life. And with this comes such pride and joy that he was able to complete the journey as intended, as tailor-made to his specific instructions and assisted at all times by his loving Spirit team.

There are optional exit points – escape clauses, in a manner of speaking – open to us in our contracts of life. My Grandfather could have opted out at any time but he didn't, and his Soul advanced in the wisdom of the great knowledge that was gained. Such superb knowledge of the human condition! Awareness of immense physical pain and suffering, knowledge of the endurance and physical limitations of the human body, and the understanding of life and of lingering death – this knowledge will complete us. Such advanced learnings of a wise, old Soul.

I tell of my Grandfather's journey not to cause

distress to anyone, but to highlight the success and grandeur of a simple life lived in dignity and strength. And yet we all have our own success stories! We have endured much in the progress of our Souls over many eons, so never overlook how far you have come on your journey of the Soul. You are so much more powerful and courageous than you will ever realise. Never forget where you are from and where you belong – as one with God and the 'I AM', the *source of all that is*.

My Grandfather is certainly an inspiration to me, just as most lives are indeed inspirational, yet unfortunately most of us are not privy to the progress of another's Soul journey. Neither the small steps, nor the great leaps and bounds made in the many ordinary, yet humbling lives being lived amongst us are clearly visible to most of us while our Earth-blinkers are on. If they were visible, I can guarantee that you would be on your knees in veneration of them all without a doubt, praising the quiet dignity and perseverance of your neighbour in a life lived in pure harmony of the Soul. Such love, joy and forgiveness to all – now that's a life worth living!

My Grandfather is back on the Earth again in the body of his choice learning yet another advanced lesson of the Soul, this time involving very different, but difficult, life challenges of a non-physical nature. I am truly blessed and honoured to be privy to this information and to be able to communicate with him in Spirit. My love for him is unconditional. We have shared many lifetimes on our Soul journeys through the Ages and I am in awe of what he has achieved and the difficult life lessons he has elected to undertake on the journey of his Soul. This knowledge brings me such joy and my heart bursts with pride at his achievements.

So at this point I encourage you to really start to think about what exactly this all means to you on your journey of the Soul and in your understanding of the greater purpose of your life. What are your goals? Go within, sit in quiet contemplation and you will gain a sense of where you want to be, what brings you pride and joy, and the direction you need to go in life.

Of course you will not be privy to the circumstances of your planned passing (although some privileged Souls are provided this knowledge – yet again another test of the Soul). If we knew what was to befall us we would likely live in the utmost fear and panic every day and squander our chance to live life to the fullest.

Do not take a back seat in life. Do not be a passenger waiting for others to provide directions and call the shots. It is your life, your chance to grow. Push yourself forward out of comfort zones. Seize the day and let no-one diminish you. You are much more than you could possibly ever believe; you are greater than you will ever know and you have travelled further on this voyage of the Soul than you could ever anticipate.

Do not ever sell yourself short. You have many untapped skills and capabilities. Be proud of who you are. Do not live with self-doubt or self-loathing. Know always that you are special. You are unique and irreplaceable and you will never live this exact, inimitable life again so make every second count in this short life on planet Earth.

Do not put your life on hold until some imaginary future date or milestone. Do not wait to be rich enough, powerful enough, successful enough or happy enough before you plan to truly start living the life you want to live. Don't live somebody else's life by proxy. Refocus your time and energies on what you know deep down are the most important things in life to you. If you follow your heart, you can't go wrong.

It is the simple things in life that will bring the most joy – family, friends, animals, birdsong, nature, art, music, laughter and above all, helping others. To bring joy, love and understanding into someone else's life benefits the giver more than the receiver. We all need the means to live and to fund the basic necessities of life, but do not focus on making money to the detriment of all else, foregoing all that is worthy and sustaining in our lives. Death bed regrets are the sour taste of a life squandered.

Do not let your ego misguide you. We are all the same; we are all living in quiet desperation until finally the penny drops and the truth does set us free. Believe in love, believe in Spirit, and the wonders of the universe will be available to you. And all power to you as the tried and tested Captain of Your Soul.

6.
A Life to be proud of

Two people I know well, a couple, have been linked to each other through many lifetimes. As mentioned previously, this type of link is the normal state of affairs, as we are all part of a wider Soul group and reincarnate together in many lifetimes. One partner of this particular couple is a highly moral and ethical person who happens to be an atheist who takes no stock in the journey of the Soul or the existence of Spirit. In their view, dead is dead and dust is dust and no further discussions need be had. The other partner believes in God and the existence of Spirit. A stalemate has occurred, a truce of sorts where the topic of life after death is rarely discussed. If it is, the opposing views are tolerated but usually with some degree of derision on both sides.

A major lesson for the couple in this life relates to respect and acceptance of the other partner's views and belief systems. Both are required to let go of the pain, disappointment and feelings of betrayal caused by their beliefs not being validated by the other. For both, this pain has created a heavy burden which has carried through the Ages. They both feel disrespected despite the deep bonds of love they feel for each other.

As a Medium, the baggage of their Souls presents to me as burdens of 'rejection' accumulated in similar situations over many lifetimes. They are, each of them, both the rejecter and the rejected. The looking glass presents to each the parts, but they fail to see the reflection as a whole.

To release this emotional baggage, indeed any baggage, involves a conscious decision to let all pain and disappointment go. Release it. All expectations, all judgement, all pain and longing – give it up to the universe to transmute into love and light with wisdom and understanding. Make this the same fate of any lingering pain and sorrow, even if you find it hard to identify the source. Let go and let God. Express postage; do not return to sender.

How is this done? Well, it is all about your intentions; your thought patterns are the key. The right intentions will see you far on your journey of the Soul. Intend to cleanse your Soul of pain and sorrow and you are well on the way to lightness of being – a blessing to be sure.

Understand that the roots of your pain may run far deeper than you will ever know, as most of us will be unaware of the excess baggage of the Soul which serves to magnify the sorrow. The clue to the size of your karmic burden will be if the current life issue brings you disproportionate pain and heartache in comparison to its true magnitude or significance.

Scenarios involving rejection of others play out in many a life plan, as too does rejection of self. Failure to accept all others with dignity and grace and respect them for who they are is a failure to fully empathise with your fellow human beings. This represents an inability to fully understand the human condition in all its glory.

The journey of faith is a matter of the heart, not the head, and all must find their own way in their search for the eternal truth of their existence. Beliefs cannot be forced upon another and each person must decide what sits well in their heart. This is a private matter (unless it harms another) which should not be open to another's ridicule or scrutiny.

Many sceptics go out of their way to counter an adherent's claims of a particular faith or belief system in God. They argue that science and rational minds are contrary to religious beliefs, and that people of faith are simple-minded sheep to follow such dogma unquestioningly. However, belief in God and belief in science are not mutually exclusive views. But doubt is the way of the world. It is not *what* we have forgotten; it is that we have forgotten that we have forgotten! In faith and in trust, many a truth seeker will find the elusive Holy Grail of wisdom and set sail on the ship of destiny, with love in their hearts and fulfilment in their souls.

It is true, as often claimed, that there has been

much widespread suffering over the centuries due to religious beliefs of some form or other, and critics often highlight this issue in their assertion that humankind is better off without religion. But as humankind evolves rapidly on all levels – socially, technologically and scientifically – spiritual faith becomes as necessary to life as oxygen, food and water. And those left behind will find that the nose-bag of history will provide no sustenance to the emptiness of their life.

Understanding the human condition brings empathy and empathy brings understanding. Thus we move closer to the knowledge that we are all equal on our journey home to the Creator, no matter what name we give our God or what form he or she takes. Acceptance of difference is what I speak of, and non-judgement of others is the song-sheet we need to sing from. Non-judgement is not about condoning a crime, absolving unethical behaviours or providing amnesty for another's sins; it is about unconditional love of all others.

To belittle a person's life choices, beliefs or identity because they differ from yours is to judge another. Many fail this test again and again in the lesson page of their life. To judge another based on hegemony is to place a yoke firmly around your neck and walk lockstep down the tunnel of life, no view to call your own.

To denounce another person or a group of people publicly or privately simply because they are different to you – when truth be known we are each of us an enigma – is to stain your Soul with spite. To secretly harbour disrespect of a person for their colour, creed, disability, gender identity or sexual orientation due to religious dogma or some bias or other that you have absorbed, is to judge another. We are all of us equal in Spirit. Who are we to judge another Soul's sacred journey and the circumstances of their lives?

It is easy to be kind when life is going well. It is when we are tested that our polite and civilised facade starts to melt away. Our patience wanes, our manner is rude, and our obstinacy is laid bare for all to see. Survivors of atrocities know only too well the thin veneer between civilised and brutish, and many people recognise humankind's potential for evil. They are under no illusions as to the true depths a person can sink when barbarity rules, greed and self-interest reign supreme, and compassion flies out the window.

Unless you are seriously tested in life you never really know how you will fare. Would you sacrifice your life to save another or save yourself first? Would you go hungry so others could eat? Would you speak out at injustices or turn the other way? Many are tested in this way and depart their physical life with flying colours; their name forever emblazoned on the Honour Board of Love, their actions embossed in gold in the Book of Life. The glory of their passing is a true prize for the Soul.

Some people appear to live a life of normalcy whilst harbouring the darkest secrets of their hidden world. Child abusers, traffickers of human misery, rapists, trolls and plotters, kidnappers, blackmailers and fraudsters galore; there appears no limit to the hypocrisy of their lives. Pain is inflicted on others without empathy or care, a truly miserable state of affairs where innocence dies, hearts are deadened, and the light rarely shines.

There are no secrets in the Spirit world. All is known, all is understood. All one's actions, thoughts and words are laid bare. All is recorded in the Record Book of Life, the hypocrisy writ large.

Others don't even bother to hide their true ways. Their hate is tangible, their arrogance brazen, and their life as purveyors of cruelty, pain and suffering is on show for all to see. Violent crusaders, these poor Souls take the long way home. Their Soul's precarious pathway full of minefields, chasms and dead-end streets is a heavy price to be paid for sure. Their life journey is tortuous and their baggage complete with the full weight of the horrors of the Ages dragged along behind them.

Pity their free will choices but send them love as they languish in the wilderness of their Soul. Shine your light for all to see and it will help raise the energetic vibration wherever you go. You can do this by living through your heart centre in all that you do, loving all others unconditionally, and rising above pettiness and spite. Your light – the divine light of righteousness – will shine brightly. Your light will help to activate the light of others on a deeper level of consciousness, and the world will be a far better place.

Remember this – if the heartbreak of the world seeks to cripple you, always look at the bigger picture. Many tragedies occur and when innocents are deliberately slaughtered in cold blood it is easy to drown in the heartache of precious life so wantonly destroyed. We try to block it out but it invades our world, a blanket of grief settling on our collective hearts and minds. The sorrow permeates our very being. It is vital to always believe that much good can arise from the ashes of hate. Communities unite in suffering and bloodshed. There is an overwhelming expression of love and solidarity for the victims and their loved ones. Understand that this will help to negate the evil perpetrated.

Evil cannot thrive in the higher vibration of love. The outpouring of compassion, love and harmony indeed raises the vibration of our world, promoting an increased acceptance and love of all of humanity. These noble Souls have sacrificed much so that all of humanity can grow. This is consciousness raising on a mass scale.

Each of us tries our best as we go about our lives, yet still we unintentionally manage to hurt others with our actions, thoughts and words – especially our words. Try as we might, words once spoken cannot be unspoken. Hurt is inflicted, pain is inevitable, and we continue on our merry way, vowing to try harder next time. In this way we learn and we grow, we forgive and we mature.

Tragic accidents occur and many lives are changed in an instant. Remorse is boundless, life goes on, and we all understand that no-one is immune to the vagaries of life. Accidents are part and parcel of the human condition and a stark reminder to all that every day is precious.

It is all about our intentions in life. Accidents are accidents. Malicious, cruel and nasty behaviour, however, is a whole other category. Do not be the person that harbours evil in your wake. Do not make those deliberate choices that add to the pain and hatred of the world. You will wallow in a prison of your own making, with hate and fear the bars of choice and sorrow and pain the locksmith's keys.

You know this is the truth, no matter the strength of your denials, the gumption of your bravado and your concentrated efforts to bury your unease. The discomfort and guilt seeks to swallow you whole. Oh pitiful and horrible night! How uneasily you turn in your sleep, the morning a blessed relief to the dreams that haunt you.

It is far easier to ignore the disquiet you have buried deep within your psyche when you are younger and busily amused with the many distractions of life. But come old age, when the pace of activity slows and introspection becomes the default setting of life, the memories will haunt and the burden grows a tail.

Look to the light and it will guide you home. It is never too late to change your ways. Vow to change. Seek forgiveness, do good deeds, forgive yourself and move on. What's ruined is ruined, do not linger there. Begin again, start afresh and redeem yourself with love. A true conversion of the Soul, a resurrection of a life, a transformation to be proud of – this is your ticket to joy and everlasting happiness. It means that a lesson has been learned.

Of course you will still be disappointed with any major misdeeds in life and the evil choices that you made. Were you a murderer, or a child abuser? Well then, of course there will be regrets.

On your return to Spirit you will review and judge every word, thought and action in the Record Book of Life and you will see the consequences of your choices reverberating throughout the universe, like a ripple from a stone thrown in a pond. You will feel shame, horror and pain at the truth of your legacy. Even so, God forgives all and your Spirit team loves you unconditionally.

So forgive yourself now, make amends, and have true contrition for your Soul. You will pass over with one less regret, and you will have much to be proud of in that you saw the errors of your ways and sought redemption for your Soul. This is indeed a coming of age and the joyful truth of your existence will come to bear upon your Soul.

This is what dreams are made of.

7.
Conclusion

Is there really any great difference to bemoan in where or how people pray, which traditions are followed, where or how their bodies are finally laid to rest, or even what name they give their God? It is our humanity that unites us, and our religions that divide us. Judgement is a loveless act. Do not get caught up in judging others as being inferior to your own good self.

Rightly or wrongly, we are social by nature and tribalism compels us, but we must remember always that we are eternal Spirit living a physical existence and we are all equal in matters of the Soul. We must not wring our hands and shake our heads and feed into the circus when we ourselves are far from perfect. Do not be swayed to judge another, lest the story begins another way, another day, where the *judge* becomes the *judged* and all will take their turn in the storybook of life.

To be righteous is to have unconditional love for all, and this will ensure that your heart is always open. You never judge another's choices as you have an innate understanding that all life paths cross treacherous ground and who are you to judge? Many a Parson's nose upturned in sanctimonious judgement soon enough becomes a Fowl's rump when serendipity follows them home.

You know that you will be tested in life – there is no denying that fact. When you fully understand the purpose of your life on Earth so much of your life will make sense to you. You will reflect on your life thus far and realise what was missing. You will understand that there is no turning back from love; unconditional love in all its glory.

To live a pure life in *righteousness of being* is to feel in harmony with all others and with all God's creatures on Earth. This provides a true feeling of peace and contentment that nothing can destroy. You will rise above all heartache and sorrow. You will understand that life is fleeting and you need to make the most of every living moment on Earth.

Never think you can love too much, or give too much of yourself to others. There can never be too much love. Love is the lifeblood of the universe. This cannot be overstated; love is the great energetic force that sustains and transcends all.

So for all your worries and for all your doubts, vow to view your life differently from now on. Embrace each situation that presents as an opportunity for growth. Seize the chance to make choices you are proud of – choices about your actions, thoughts and words as you go about your daily life.

View all adversaries as your teachers, and be thankful for the gift of learning they are presenting to you. At your reunion in Spirit you will look back on your life with glee as you all once again gather to compare notes, celebrate the results of your tests, and honour the parts you just played in the roles of your lives. A Study Group of the highest calibre!

Never deem your life as insignificant. It is not of consequence that you weren't a freedom fighter or humanitarian of the century. You may not have discovered a vaccine to eradicate suffering, nor won a Nobel peace prize. But this is irrelevant to the success of your life and the progress of your Soul. You may think you didn't save the world, but it is the everyday small kindnesses that make your life worthwhile and do, in fact, save the world with love.

When you view your humble, yet righteous, life from the vantage point of the Spirit realms, it will be the smallest things that will amaze you when you see their energetic effect on the world around you. There will be no greed, selfishness, hate or spite recorded in your Book of Life. It will be full of everyday acts of love, kindness, mercy and compassion; many of which may have seemed insignificant to you at the time. This will be the crowning glory of your *Life Review,* and you will be so full of pride. Such honour and glory for your Soul!

So remember this: not everyone has the chance to be a Queen or a President. Nor is everyone in a position where they can eradicate slavery or ease poverty and inequality (although many do squander their chances to make a difference in this regard). Onerous decisions on warfare and peace may be required by those in power but, unsurprisingly, not every life plan or contract has such arduous and weighty clauses attached. The brave Souls that do elect such challenging roles when planning their incarnations are truly courageous, no matter if they fail their tests of righteousness due to greed, power or corruption. Their fortitude and resilience will see them proud.

So next time you feel animosity towards someone in politics or in power, nod and bow in appreciation of the journey of their Soul, for God truly knows how hard it is. And it is a double-edged sword if their well-developed ego – often a requirement to get them into power in the first place – completely disconnects them from their heart centre, thus providing a hindrance and a limitation on their pathway. This is tenfold of baggage to be sure.

In every life there are many, many chances to progress your Soul and prove yourself to God, in big ways and small. You are being healed and nurtured, and Spirit are indeed watching over you. Your loved ones in Spirit who passed over before you are all active on the sidelines of your life, cheering you on from the boundary. They want your life to be a success, bathed in the glory of love. So persevere in your life with dignity and in grace, and let no-one bring you down.

Love like there is no tomorrow. For you are loved, and you *are* love; you are a blessing to the world. The Angels unite to soothe the world with love. Look to the heavens, they applaud you. And glory knows your name.

This has been decreed.

8.
Personal Message and Prayer

A few months prior to starting this book my wonderful Spirit team provided me with this exquisite message of inspiration, followed by the beautiful words of what was revealed to be a prayer. You will note the prayer starts in a familiar fashion of 'The Lord is my Shepherd'. I suspect Spirit specifically organised the prayer in this way so that I would more easily recognise it as a prayer. Otherwise, it may have gone unnoticed in the densely scribbled entries of my diary.

The prayer is so lovingly worded and structured that I was inspired to share it. It is a simple prayer which gives us the hope and joy of Jesus returning once again to teach the world of love and forgiveness. The wonder of the Christ Light is set to once more illuminate the world. (I need to mention here that this return will not be in the way of old that many are expecting.) So we watch and wait, and we are not forgotten. We must await this time with open hearts and open minds, and the world will surely be a better place. Rejoice!

* * *

Personal message to me from my Spirit Guides: The way is known, the path complete. In loving haste you tread righteously to your goal – the purification of Spirit and unification of your Soul. You know the joy, the sublime wonder of the heart. We reach out to you, our loving arms embrace you, for you are known to us and wise your heart be. Round and round the universe we seek you out and the Angels do declare: come forth with the Word to set them free.

Prosper those who take the hand of God and lead where they may follow. Prosper all who know God's Word and provide sustenance to the masses. The time has come for greatness of Spirit; the truth be known by few. Go in peace and redeem your heart of hearts, for it is a lonely path to take when non-believers pull you down and nary a thought to be had of Christendom's demise.

Talk the talk, walk the walk, and you will find that the time is now to come into the wilderness and shout your message to the treetops:

The Lord is my Shepherd and I shall not want.

*He leads me from the wilderness
and glory be thy name.*

*He comes again to spread the word of love, and
none so wise as those who look into the eyes of
love and declare "it was ever so".*

*Glory to you our Master on High,
we will not forsake you.*

*We welcome you with open arms and carry your
message of love far and wide.*

The Holy are gathered, awaiting the good news.

Oh Father in Heaven, we beseech you.

Have mercy on our Souls and send the gift of love,

for mankind is weary and loveless, and in pain.

*The Light will shine forever more and
all will be forgiven.*

Hallelujah.

Epilogue

We must remember who we are. We must know that all our summers will count for naught if we fail to open our hearts and minds and sing the song of love.

Love is the song to make all pain retreat; the song to show us how to live and how to feed the Soul. For the Soul hungers, don't you see? It is the hunger of an almighty need for sustenance of life and sustenance of the divine. It is the thirst of knowledge, deep and true; and the thirst of forgiveness, staid and clear.

Strong is the Valley of my Heart, for the furrows of time doth weaken but the essence of the soil is lush and fertile once more. Go within, act in goodness and grace and forgiveness to all, and you will find that all is as it should be. The rivers are mined, the valleys are ploughed, but green is the Valley of your Soul.

www.ingramcontent.com/pod-product-compliance
Lightning Source LLC
LaVergne TN
LVHW091315080426
835510LV00007B/508